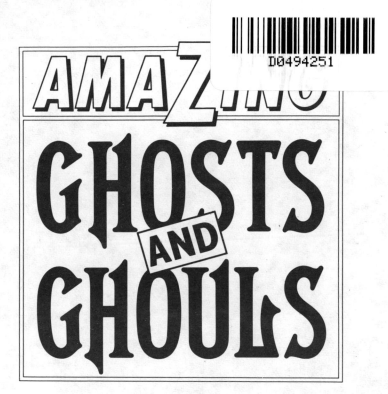

AMAZING
GHOSTS AND GHOULS

PETER ELDIN
ILLUSTRATED BY KIM BLUNDELL

First published in 1987 by
Octopus Books Limited
59 Grosvenor Street
London, W1

Text by Peter Eldin, Data Forum Ltd
Illustrated by Kim Blundell
Cover by Mik Brown

ISBN 0 7064 2904 4

Printed in the United Kingdom

Introduction

Have you ever heard the mysterious chanting at Beaulieu Abbey or the sound of the ghostly army at Souter Fell? Did you ever see the headless ghost of Anne Boleyn or the phantom hitch-hiker of Holcombe Rogus?

If you haven't – hold on to your seat! This book is crammed with ghosts and ghouls of all kinds: ghosts from the depths of the sea, royal ghosts, meddlesome poltergeists, ghosts that haunt houses, theatres, castles and graveyards, animal ghosts, phantom skulls and ghoulish skeletons.

Are your nerves strong enough? Read, on and find out.

The Headless Lady

A s he was driving near St James's Park in London one morning in 1975, a taxi driver saw a headless woman crossing the road in front of him. When he reported the sighting he was told that he had seen the ghost of an 18th-century woman who had been beheaded by her husband. The murderous husband had then thrown his wife's body into the lake in St James's Park.

The Black Hound of Odin

A n enormous black dog is said to haunt Gatcombe, the home of Princess Anne. The dog is thought to be the black hound of Odin, a viking warrior who plundered the area 1000 years ago.

Cast the Lead, Sir

I n the early years of this century, a sailor on *HMS Society* was drowned. A few nights later the captain was woken up by the sailor's ghost. 'Cast the lead, sir!' said the apparition. Then it vanished.

The captain did as he had been instructed, and found that his ship was off course and sailing in only 10 metres (36 feet) of water. The ghost had prevented the ship from running aground.

Awd Nance

A wd (Old) Nance is the name of a skull that refuses to leave Burton Agnes Hall in Yorkshire, northern England. It has been there for over 300 years. Every time someone tries to remove it, terrifying groans are heard throughout the house, together with scratching noises, shuffling sounds and slamming doors.

Apparition of an Admiral

O n 22 June, 1893, a number of guests gathered for tea at the London home of Vice-Admiral Sir George and Lady Tyron. When the admiral, in full dress uniform, walked down the stairs and out of the door his wife screamed in horror. The guests were also surprised, for they knew that the admiral was not even in London at the time. He was miles away, on board his ship *Victoria*, off the coast of Tripoli. What none of them could possibly realize was that at that very moment the *Victoria* was going down with over half its officers and men. Sir George was among the many who perished.

Spirits in the Air

Captain Robert Loft and Second Officer Don Repo died when their Eastern Airlines L-1011 TriStar crashed in Southern Florida on 29 December, 1972. But their ghosts were seen for quite some time afterwards. The first sighting was made by one of the airline's vice-presidents. He was chatting to a uniformed pilot on a flight to San Francisco when he suddenly realized he was talking to Captain Loft. The figure then vanished.

In February, 1974, on a flight to Mexico City, a stewardess saw Don Repo. She mentioned this to the flight engineer who said that he, too, had seen him. He said Repo had warned him to watch out for fire on the plane. Sure enough, when the plane took off from Mexico City, one of the engines burst into flames. Fortunately, the fire was quickly put out.

The two men were seen on several other flights during 1974 but have not been seen since.

Death of a Singer

I n 1905 a lady singer, whose career had not been very successful, decided to kill herself. She climbed on to the roof of a theatre in Clapham, London, and started to sing dramatically. Then she fell through the skylight, to her death. She has been seen in the theatre several times since, and her plaintiff song has even been recorded on tape.

Queen in the Library

I n 1897, the Officer of the Guard at Windsor Castle, Lieutenant Carr Glynn, claimed he saw the ghost of Queen Elizabeth I. She was strolling in the Royal Library. The officer was not the only person to have seen her. Queen Victoria's eldest daughter also saw the ghost of the former queen as have many other people since.

On Guard at Windsor

In the early 1970s, a guardsman on duty at Windsor Castle in England reported seeing the ghost of a policeman. The ghost was seen at the very spot where a policeman had died in the 1920s, and it has been sighted several times since.

Jane Seymour at Hampton Court

The ghost of Jane Seymour, the third and beloved wife of King Henry VIII, makes a regular appearance at Hampton Court Palace, the former permanent Royal Family residence just outside London. She glides through the passageways every 12 October, the anniversary of the birth of her son, Edward, in 1537.

The Ethereal Choir

Mrs Gertrude Gould was walking past Bramshott Court, a mansion near Liphook, Hampshire, southern England, one evening in 1946, when she heard '. . . a glorious male-voice choir which came nearer and nearer until it seemed to be over my head.' Noticing that the words were sung in Latin, Mrs Gould assumed that she was hearing a radio playing. But the only radio at Bramshott Court was broken, and the nearest one was in the village, some distance away.

One wing of the old mansion had once been a monastery. Was it the voices of long-dead monks that Mrs Gould heard that evening?

Death of an Actor

On 16 December, 1897, the actor, William Terris, was stabbed on his way to the Adelphi Theatre in the Strand, London. His ghost has been seen in the theatre several times since.

The Creature of Croglin

For one glorious year Edward Cranswell was very pleased with his new house, Croglin Hall in England. But he changed his mind during the summer of 1875. His sister, Amelia, was unable to sleep one night and was sitting gazing out at the garden. As she watched, a strange, dog-like skeleton came across the lawn and began scratching at the window.

Amelia screamed with terror and ran to the door. But it was locked. In her panic she dropped the key and could not find it in the dark. She could hear her two brothers pounding on her door but, by now, the skeleton had removed a pane of glass. A bony arm came through the broken pane and began to open the window.

When her brothers eventually managed to open the door they found Amelia unconscious on the floor. Blood was pouring from terrible wounds on her throat, face and shoulders. Her brother Michael saw the skeleton running away.

After a long convalescence in Switzerland, Amelia returned to Croglin Hall in spite of her brothers' misgivings. For, during her absence, there had been other reports in the area of girls being attacked by a strange creature.

It was not long after that the skeleton appeared once again at Croglin. But this time, Amelia's brothers were prepared. They now slept near to Amelia's bedroom and ruled that none of the doors were to be locked. When they heard Amelia's terrified screams, Michael dashed to her room and Edward headed for the front door. The skeleton ran away towards the churchyard. As it scrambled over the churchyard wall Edward fired his pistol. The creature staggered for a moment and then slowly began to make its way to the family vault of the Fishers – the family who had owned Croglin before the Cranswells.

Next day the brothers took some local men and broke into the vault. Every coffin was broken and the pieces were strewn across the floor. Only one coffin was intact. They opened the coffin and found a shrivelled, dog-like creature inside. It had a flesh wound in its leg! The villagers agreed that the corpse should be burnt, and the terror of Croglin Hall was never seen again.

13

The Dancing Ghost

A most unusual ghost has been reported at Honor Oak Park in Dulwich, south London. Near One-Tree Hill there is a large cemetery, and it is here that the ghost of a young girl appears.

She is said to be in her late teens, and she has long blonde hair. Unlike most ghosts, this young lady appears to be quite content, for she is often seen dancing happily.

Coach of the Devil

T he 17th-century Scottish nobleman, Andrew Skene, was reputed to have dabbled in the occult arts. Everywhere he went he was accompanied by four birds – a crow, a magpie, a jackdaw and a hawk. These birds were said to be fed on the carcasses of dead bodies dug up from Skene churchyard.

One New Year's Eve, Skene ordered his coach-man to drive across the surface of the Loch of

Skene. (He had conjured up a layer of ice so the coach could do so.) He told the coachman that he must not, under any circumstances, look back, but drive across the Loch and head straight for the Hill of Fare on the opposite bank.

They made the journey across the Loch safely, but as they reached the shore on the other side, the coachman could not resist looking behind him. There, sitting next to Andrew Skene, the coachman saw the Devil!

It is said that every 31 December since then, a ghostly coach has been seen racing across the Loch of Skene.

The Dartmoor Shepherd

David Davies spent 50 years in Dartmoor Prison in Devon. He was given the job of looking after the sheep, and they nicknamed him 'The Dartmoor Shepherd'. Davies died in 1929, but he can still be seen herding his sheep through the Dartmoor mists.

15

Pact with the Devil

According to legend, a girl at Potter Heigham in Norfolk sold her soul to the Devil in the year 1742. She was carried off in a coach by demons, but the coach crashed as it crossed a bridge and all the occupants fell into the river. Each year, on 31 May, a phantom coach driven by a skeleton is said to pass over the bridge.

Bells in the Abbey

Although Rievaulx Abbey, near York, England, was abandoned in 1539 and is now a roofless shell, a heavenly choir has been heard there many times and a bell is sometimes heard ringing. But there has not been a real bell in the abbey for over 400 years!

Ghost Army

I n 1745, a ghostly army was seen walking across Souter Fell in the Lake District in the north of England. This was considered rather unusual, for there had never been a battle in the area, and there was no reason for an army to be marching there. Even stranger was the following report of the sight:

'Carriages were now interspersed with troops; and everybody knew that no carriage had been, or could be, on the summit of Souter Fell. The multitude was beyond imagination for the troops filled a space of half a mile, and marched quickly till night hid them – still marching. There was nothing vaporous or indistinct about the appearance of these spectres. So real did they seem that some of the people went up the next morning to look for the hoof-marks of the horses; and awful it was to them to find not one footprint on heather or grass.'

Back Through Time

I n 1901, two English women visiting Versailles Palace in France were surprised when they saw people walking about dressed in 18th-century costume. Whilst visiting the Petit Trianon, in which the ill-fated Marie Antoinette had lived, the two women had apparently stepped back in time, to the year 1770.

Ghost in the Hotel

R adio announcer, Ray Moore, was up at 4.30 a.m. on a cold January morning in 1971. He was presenting an early morning show and was staying at the Langham Hotel, conveniently placed just over the road from the BBC studios, in London. He stepped out on to his hotel room balcony, hoping the chilly air would help him to wake up, and noticed a figure at the window of the floor above. It was that of a big man, wearing a uniform, and there seemed to be a glow emanating from his body.

When he went downstairs, Moore mentioned this strange apparition to the commissionaire. He was told that it was the ghost of a German officer who had killed himself just before the start of the First World War, by jumping out of the hotel window. Several other BBC personnel who have stayed in the same room on other occasions have also seen the ghost.

The Cavalier of Salisbury Hall

Salisbury Hall, near London Colney, Hertfordshire, England, was the Royalists' headquarters during the English Civil War (1642-49). One Royalist Cavalier still lives there! He was delivering despatches when he was spotted by a group of Roundheads. He dived into the hall and searched for somewhere to hide. When the Roundheads entered the building, he realized there was no escape and he killed himself by piercing himself with his sword. His ghost, with a sword sticking through him, now haunts the house.

Businessman in a Bowler

On 2 March, 1948, a DC3 aeroplane crashed on the runway at London's Heathrow airport. Twenty-two passengers, mainly businessmen, were killed. Since that day, a man in a bowler hat has been seen several times standing on the runway.

Anne Boleyn's Gallop

At midnight on the anniversary of her execution, 19 May, 1536, the ghost of Anne Boleyn travels from the Tower of London to Blickling Hall in Norfolk. She rides in a phantom coach, driven by headless coachmen and pulled by headless horses. Anne herself sits inside. She, too, is headless.

The Old Lady of The New Theatre

The ghost of an old lady is often seen in the Royal Box of The New Theatre in Cardiff, Wales. She usually appears to be searching for something. Then she walks down the stairs towards the stalls. At a matinee performance long ago, a woman was found dead in the Royal Box — it is believed that it is her ghost that haunts the theatre.

King at the Seaside

King George IV (1762-1830) was an extravagant and generous patron of the arts. He built a vast, ornate palace at his favourite seaside resort of Brighton, in the south of England. The palace, known as the Brighton Pavilion, was stocked with priceless art treasures and was the scene of dazzling and fashionable parties. Now the king's ghost roams the halls of the Pavilion.

Vengeful Skulls

When Myles Phillipson, a magistrate, moved into his new house, Calgarth Hall, in the Lake District in northern England, he invited all his friends to a house-warming party. The party was in full swing when, suddenly, the guests heard Phillipson's wife scream. They found her on the staircase staring at two grinning skulls.

Phillipson took the skulls and threw them out of the house, but during the night the skulls reappeared on the staircase. In the days that followed, Phillipson tried every means to get rid of the skulls, but no matter what he did they always returned.

News of the menacing skulls quickly spread, and soon Phillipson found that his business was in financial trouble. Over the next few months, his wealth steadily diminished until he was left virtually penniless. Finally, Phillipson died, a broken man.

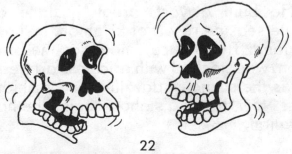

It turned out that the two skulls were those of a man and his wife who had previously owned Calgarth Hall. Phillipson had desired to own the property so much that he had had them executed for a crime they had not committed.

On the night of the magistrate's death, the skulls could be heard laughing throughout the house. They had had their revenge at last.

Headless King

A headless ghost has often been seen at Maple Hall in Cheshire, England. It is thought to be the ghost of King Charles I who was beheaded in 1649.

The Lady of Glamis

I n 1540, the wife of the 6th Lord Glamis was burned as a witch. Today her ghost haunts Glamis Castle in Scotland, where she has been seen by the Queen Mother amongst others.

The Faceless Miner

Stephen Dimbleby was a miner at Silverwood Colliery, South Yorkshire. One evening in 1982, his colleagues were alarmed to see him rush out of the mine, screaming and crying, into the arms of an amazed pit deputy.

Later, Dimbleby recovered sufficiently to relate what had happened. He had been walking towards the coal seam to start his shift when he saw a shadowy figure ahead of him. At first he thought it was one of his colleagues – and then he realized there should not have been anyone else in that part of the mine at that time of night. The figure was wearing a waistcoat and a grubby shirt and had an old-fashioned square helmet with a light on it. The young miner lifted his lamp to get a better look at the man, and then froze in his tracks – the figure had no face!

The pit deputy later revealed that several other miners had reported similar strange sightings in the same area. Coal Board officials then confirmed that a miner had been killed at that spot in 1968, when he was trapped in a coal-cutting machine. At that time miners wore exactly the type of clothing that Stephen Dimbleby had so vividly described!

Washing Away the Blood

A lady with a black face and hands and wearing a long white dress haunts Bisham Abbey, near Marlow in Buckinghamshire, England. She always seems to be washing her hands. It is said that this is the ghost of Lady Elizabeth Hoby, the wife of one of Queen Mary's courtiers, who murdered her son. Even now, her spirit is still trying to wash her baby's blood from her hands.

The Polite Ghost

T he ghost of a nun knocks on the bedroom doors in Ripley Castle, Yorkshire. But she is very polite. She only enters the room if the occupant calls: 'Come in'.

The Poltergeist of Barking Creek

J ohn Willis and his wife Rosemary were watching television one evening at their home in Barking, Essex, when suddenly they heard the sound of loud crashing and banging coming from their children's room. The couple looked up in alarm and rushed upstairs to find out what was wrong. As they entered the bedroom, an ornament crashed against the wall, narrowly missing Rosemary's head. The room itself seemed alive with activity. Bedding and toys were flying around the room. Cowering together in the corner were their children, ten-year-old Terry and seven-year-old Sandra, terrified out of their wits.

The two children were hastily bundled out of the room, and the bedroom door was slammed shut. All four stood on the landing shaking with fear and unable to understand what strange phenomenon could be responsible for what they had witnessed in the room.

From July to September, 1952, the Willis family had to endure a continuous barrage of similar happenings in their house. Objects flew around rooms, a kitchen table split in half as the family looked on, an iron poker was bent in half, and the sitting-room curtains were ripped to shreds by unseen hands.

26

Although no one in the house was ever hurt by the poltergeist, Norman Horridge, an expert on the paranormal was convinced that a strange and evil force existed in the house, and persuaded the Willis family to agree to an exorcism.

The exorcism was carried out in September, 1952. Doors blew open and banged to and fro, as if the poltergeist was angry at being banished. Finally, the house went quiet — the poltergeist had departed for ever.

Royal Library Visitor

T he ghost of King Charles I, of England, who was beheaded in 1649, has often been seen standing by a table in the library at Windsor Castle in Berkshire.

Accident in Time

In the early 1960s, a car plunged into the Kyle of Lochalsh, Scotland, and its occupants were drowned. The car was identical to a phantom car that had been sighted regularly in the region for over 20 years. After the accident, the ghost vehicle was never seen again.

Walking the Ramparts

A famous ghost has often been seen walking the ramparts between the Queen's House and the Bloody Tower at the Tower of London. It is the ghost of Sir Walter Raleigh, the 15th-century sailor and explorer who was imprisoned in the Tower for 13 years.

The Agreement

When he was a student in Edinburgh, Scotland, Lord Brougham had a long discussion with a friend about the possibility of life after death. They reached an agreement, that whoever died first would try to contact the other from beyond the grave. When the two men completed their studies they left Edinburgh and went their separate ways.

Many years later, Brougham was stepping out of his bath when he saw his old friend sitting in a chair. He noted in his diary that the event had occurred on 19 December. A few days later a letter arrived from India, informing him that his friend had died – on 19 December.

The Horrible Nun

Early one morning, as he was driving from Chippenham to Bath, in the west of England, Laurie Newman saw a nun. He slowed down as he passed her, but as he did so, she turned and leapt at his windscreen. Her face was that of a horrible skull!

Poltergeist at Large

Many strange things happened in a house at Seaford, Long Island, USA. Bottles of medicine opened by themselves, tables fell over, and a statuette floated through the air. Investigators were baffled by the case, and to this day it is not known whether the mysterious occurrences were caused by real ghosts or just a clever conjuring trick.

Ghost at the Restaurant

During the English Civil War in the 17th century, drunken soldiers murdered a young girl at an inn at Sunbury-on-Thames in Surrey. Visitors to the building, which is now a restaurant, have been terrified by sightings of the young lady. In an attempt to restrain the ghost, 'the soldier's room', where the murder occurred, has now been locked.

Head Roll

Strange thumping noises are heard in the library at St John's College, Oxford. They are said to be made by Archbishop Laud, a former Chancellor of the University, who was executed for treason in 1645. The noises are caused by the ghost rolling his severed head along the library floor!

Quilt of Mystery

Mrs Florence Delfosse was sleeping at her mother's house in Poy Sippi, Wisconsin, USA, when she was awakened by someone tugging at the quilt on her bed. She opened her eyes, but there was no one in the room. Then she heard a voice cry, 'Give me my Christmas quilt!' For three hours she struggled with the unseen

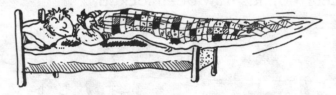

person until, eventually, the quilt became still once again and Mrs Delfosse was able to get back to sleep.

When she told her family of this strange occurrence her daughter's boyfriend offered to take the quilt to his house to test it. He went home to bed, and shortly after midnight the quilt began to move.

Suddenly, there was a knock at the front door. He went downstairs to answer it. There was a strange man at the door. Although it was pouring with rain, his hat and clothes were dry — and he had no face. After a few seconds the man left without saying a word.

The family never solved the mystery of the quilt. It had been found in a box in the house when Mrs Delfosse's mother had moved there in 1972. Why it moved or who was the mysterious being claiming ownership, they never discovered.

Cavaliers on the Road

Many motorists driving near Marston Moor, Yorkshire, have seen men dressed in old-fashioned clothes staggering along the roadside. They are said to be the spirits of some of the Cavaliers who fought the Roundheads at Marston Moor on 2 July, 1644 during the English Civil War.

Arrest that Ghost!

Inspector Sid Candler of London's Metropolitan Police was called out on an emergency call on 11 July, 1951. As he approached the house in Langmead Street, West Norwood, London, the Inspector vowed he would reprimand young Cecil Greenfield, who had made the emergency call, for making up tales about ghosts.

But when he met the eight members of the Greenfield family, Inspector Candler changed his mind. They were genuinely scared out of their wits. The family told him that the house had been invaded by strange flickering lights accompanied by loud noises, crashes, thumps and moans. The police stayed in the house that night, but nothing else happened.

The following night the Greenfields telephoned the police again. This time, eight constables were assigned to the house. On that night, and on subsequent visits, the police heard the noises for themselves. Apart from the noises, a shopping basket was mysteriously thrown along the hallway, cups and saucers moved of their own accord, pictures fell from the walls, a spoon rattled in the sugar bowl, lights flickered on and off by themselves, and strange footsteps were heard up and down the stairs.

Clergymen visited the house to try to exorcize the ghosts, but strange things continued to happen. Mysterious footprints appeared in the loft. They were rubbed out by the police, but reappeared the following day. A radio switched itself on, and a mattress was seen floating above one of the beds. And through it all, the noises continued unabated.

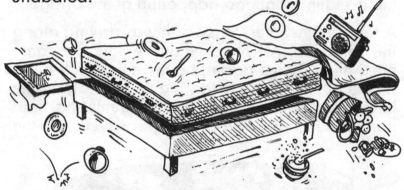

The family managed to put up with the ghostly disturbances until one morning in October, when they came down to breakfast and found that all the downstairs walls had been scribbled on. They could stand it no longer and moved house shortly after.

When new tenants moved into the house they were not once bothered by anything unusual. It seemed as if a poltergeist had been intent on getting rid of the Greenfields — and having achieved its objective it had returned to where-ver it had come from.

The Phantom Hitch-hiker

O ne evening, Harold Unsworth, a lorry driver, stopped to pick up a hitch-hiker who wanted a ride to Old Beam Bridge in Holcombe Rogus, Somerset. As they drove along, the hitch-hiker talked, in gory detail, of all the accidents that had happened at the bridge.

A few months later, Unsworth was driving along the same strip of road when he saw the same hitch-hiker. Once again, he gave the hitch-hiker a ride to Old Beam Bridge, and once again the hitch-hiker spoke about the accidents that had happened there. When they arrived. at the

bridge, the hitch-hiker got out, but asked the lorry driver to wait a few moments while he collected some belongings. The lorry driver waited for 20 minutes, but the hitch-hiker did not return, so he decided to drive on without him.

To the lorry driver's amazement, three miles further on, there in the road, stood the hitch-hiker. Suddenly, he jumped in front of the lorry. Unsworth slammed on the brakes, but although it was far too late to avoid hitting the man, he felt no impact. Unsworth looked in his rear view mirror, and saw the hitch-hiker, seemingly unharmed and waving his fist furiously at the lorry driver. Suddenly, the hitch-hiker vanished.

There was only one explanation — the man had to be a ghost. It is thought he was a victim of one of the accidents he had described so vividly.

A Mysterious Black Cat

A mysterious black cat haunts the Gateway Restaurant in Battle, Sussex, in the south of England. It has been seen by several people as it glides along a corridor before vanishing suddenly through a wall.

The Ghost Lift

I n 1969, the lift in a large hotel in Wales began to move by itself. It would rise from the ground floor and then go up to the second floor. It was first thought to be an electrical fault, but when the electricity was turned off the lift still moved. It even moved when the cables had been cut!

Ship from Nowhere

I n November, 1941, two seamen were on watch on board the American destroyer, *Kennison*, as she headed towards San Francisco, USA. Suddenly, from out of the fog, loomed an ancient two-masted sailing ship. As the vessel passed close to them, the two men could see there was absolutely no one on board. Then the ship vanished as suddenly as it had appeared.

The Haunted Golf Course

T here have been several sightings of ghosts at Howley Hall Golf Club in the West Riding of Yorkshire. Gordon Burney and his wife once saw a strange woman in a long dress appear and then vanish. Another golfer, Tom Gomersall, saw several strange-looking people at the same spot. When his dog ran towards them barking they, too, vanished.

One member of the golf club had the strange feeling that he was being watched by a crowd of people on one of the putting greens. He looked round, but there was no one to be seen.

Music from the Abbey

In 1966, Jennifer Cording was walking with a friend in Leek in Staffordshire when they heard the sound of monks chanting. Jennifer later said: 'We weren't afraid but we were surprised that such lovely music should come out of nowhere.' Although there was no rational explanation for the music they heard, the place where they walked was once the site of a Benedictine abbey.

Funeral Bells

At Lime Park in Cheshire, England, the locals often hear a strange pealing of bells. This is usually followed by the grim sight of a ghostly funeral procession. It is said to be that of a young girl who died, heartbroken, when her fiancé died at the Battle of Agincourt, in 1415.

A Grisly Sight

A female ghost is sometimes seen at the Tower of London. She is pursued by a ghostly executioner who chops off her head. The ghost is said to be that of the Countess of Salisbury, whose execution at the Tower was ordered by King Henry VIII.

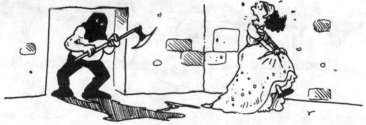

Judge Judged

The ghost of Judge John Glanville haunts Kilworthy House in Tavistock, Devon. Judge Glanville would not let his daughter, Elizabeth, marry the man she loved. Instead, she was forced to marry a goldsmith whom the judge thought more eligible. With the help of her maid and her lover, Elizabeth murdered the goldsmith. Judge Glanville sentenced his daughter and her accomplices to death. For the past 400 years, Judge Glanville has remained at Kilworthy to haunt the house as punishment for taking his daughter's life.

Herne the Hunter

For over 250 years, people have reported seeing the ghost of a man wearing antlers on his head in the Great Park at Windsor in Berkshire, England. He is Herne the Hunter, who hanged himself in the park.

The Phantom Fowl

One of the most unusual spectres on record is the ghostly chicken seen in Highgate, London. The chicken appears and then suddenly vanishes. But the strangest thing about this phantom fowl is that it is half plucked!

The Ghost of Gloucester Jail

In 1969, Robert Gore, a prisoner at Gloucester Jail, England, was so bored at Christmas that he decided to play with a glass tumbler and some letters spread over a table.

Much to his surprise, the glass suddenly began moving of its own accord. The glass moved to several of the letters in turn and spelled out the name of Jenny Godfrey. She had been murdered at that spot in the 15th century by a drunken man. The spirit of Jenny then spelled out to the prisoners several predictions of events that were about to happen. At first the prisoners scoffed, but later, when some of the predictions came true, they began to believe in the power of their spiritual contact.

There were also instances of clothes and other objects being thrown around the cells at the jail. On one occasion, one of the prisoners reported seeing a ghostly hand in his cell. Eventually, Jenny's spirit appeared less and less, but to this day strange events occur in Gloucester Jail.

The Sad Cavalier

During the English Civil War (1642-49), supporters of King Charles I, the Royalists, had to meet in secret. One group of Royalists used to meet in the cellar of the Ring O' Bells public house at Middleton, near Manchester. They were safe there until, one day, someone betrayed their hiding place to the enemy, the Roundheads.

One of the men in the cellar that day was the son of Lord Stannycliffe of Stannycliffe Hall, near Middleton. He managed to get away from the cellar and made his escape through a secret passage that led to the parish church. But the Roundheads knew about the passage and the young man was caught and killed.

Stannycliffe's body was buried under the flagstones in the cellar of the public house where he and his friends used to meet. And to this day he haunts the Ring O' Bells. He has been seen on several occasions wandering through the passageways of the building, weeping.

Even people who know nothing of the story of this ghost have reported strange events whilst visiting the Ring O' Bells. Customers have mentioned going to the bar to buy a drink, only to be pushed away by someone or something that was

not there! And the owners have often heard the sound of ghostly footsteps in the passageways.

At one time it was suggested that the cavalier's remains be removed from beneath the cellar floor and given a proper burial. But it was decided that, as the ghost did no harm, it should be allowed to remain in the building.

If you go to the Ring O' Bells today, you will find that there is still a 'cavalier's seat' in the bar and a table known as the 'ghosts table', at which Royalist ghosts are said to sit.

Singing at Beaulieu

When a villager at Beaulieu, Hampshire in southern England, dies, mysterious chanting is heard at Beaulieu Abbey. Several people have heard it, but no one can give a rational explanation for the phenomenon.

A Smelly Ghost

Footsteps have been heard frequently in Orcas Manor, near Sherborne, Dorset in southern England. The ghostly footsteps are often accompanied by a noise which sounds like a body being dragged along the ground. Even after the noise has stopped, there is a lingering, putrid smell that no one can account for.

Ghost of the Regiment

Captain Bayliss was killed in action in 1915, during the First World War, but for several years after his death he was regularly sighted by men in his regiment. He was seen astride his beautiful white charger, inspecting the camp at night. One night in 1920, a young soldier, not knowing of the ghost's nocturnal inspections, challenged the Captain. When he received no reply, the guard panicked and opened fire – and the ghost of Captain Bayliss was never seen again.

The Welcome Ghost

When a clergyman offered to exorcize the ghost from Mrs Val Williams's house in St Asaph, north Wales, she refused, saying, 'You have no right to do that. She was in this house long before we were.'

The ghost was that of a tall, thin woman wearing a white hood. Normally, the apparition, which first appeared in 1970, was seen by Val's twelve-year-old daughter, Janthea, but Val also saw her several times. Strange footsteps have also been heard around the house and objects have moved mysteriously.

Although she was a little scared by these mysterious manifestations, Mrs Williams always insisted that the ghost should be allowed to stay in the house. But who the strange lady was, or why she haunts the house, Mrs Williams and her daughter never discovered.

Headless Horse

The horrible sight of a headless horse galloping across the moors near Calverley Hall in West Yorkshire, has scared quite a number of people. The horse is said to have belonged to Walter Calverley who tried to murder all his family, and who was then executed for his crime.

Phantoms from the Deep

At Forrabury in Cornwall, residents are used to hearing the sounds of bells coming from the sea, and seeing the sight of a ghostly phantom ship.

Killer Bus

I n the Spring of 1933 a man was driving along St Mark's Road in North Kensington, London, when he suddenly saw a double-decker bus careering towards him. It was too late to avoid a collision – the bus had appeared from nowhere and all the car driver could do was to slam on his brakes and await the impact. But nothing happened. When the driver opened his eyes, the bus was nowhere in sight!

That was not the first time that the mysterious bus had been sighted. On one occasion, a driver swerved to avoid a Number 7 bus and actually crashed his car into one of the houses in the street. But when he turned to look again, the bus had disappeared.

Several other sightings of the ghostly bus were reported and a number of accidents occurred in the same street. Luckily, none of the drivers were seriously injured – until Monday, 11 June, 1933, when two cars crashed head-on, killing one of the drivers. After this fatal accident, the ghost bus disappeared for ever – perhaps satisfied that it had claimed at least one victim.

The Menacing Cavalier

During the protectorate of Oliver Cromwell in the 1650s, a fugitive Royalist, Sir Robert Earnley, died of his wounds at an inn at Sidlesham, Sussex. His two sons were hacked to death. His ghost, wearing a long coat and a three-cornered hat, now haunts the inn.

Lady of Rochester

On Good Friday 1264, a party of rebels attacked Rochester Castle in Kent and captured Lady Blanche de Warrene. Sir Ralph da Capo tried to rescue her. He fired an arrow at Sir Gilbert de Clare, one of the captors, and the arrow found its mark — but it bounced off the rebel's heavy armour and pierced the heart of Lady Blanche. Ever since, on Good Friday each year, a figure in white, her hair blowing in the breeze, glides along the battlements — an arrow pierces her heart!

The Vicar of Ratcliff Wharf

John Denning, a London builder, was mixing cement on a quay at Ratcliff Wharf in the Isle of Dogs early one morning in 1971, when he noticed an old man standing nearby. Denning said 'Good morning' to the man, but he did not reply – he just disappeared. During the days that followed, other builders on the quay also saw the man. They named him 'The Vicar', because he was dressed in a style of clothes once worn by clergymen.

Local legend tells of a vicar who ran a lodging house in the area several hundred years ago. He is said to have robbed and then murdered several of his lodgers, and he is thought to now haunt the scene of his crimes. Perhaps this accounts for the strange figure that is, to this day, seen standing on Ratcliff Wharf.

Room of Terror

One evening in September, 1912, George French and Donald Geary were returning to the farmhouse in Slieve Donard, County Down, Northern Ireland, where they were staying with friends. As they approached the building they saw that one of the upstairs rooms was on fire. Instinctively they rushed into the farmhouse to help.

The house did not burn down. In fact, there was no sign of any fire when they went upstairs to investigate. When the farmer, Mark Donague, came home he told the men: 'That room is haunted, so we always keep it locked. The last person to go in there was one of my farm workers, ten years ago. The first I knew of it was when we heard a scream. We rushed upstairs as he staggered out of the room clutching his throat. Something in that room had tried to strangle him. The key to the room has remained in my desk drawer ever since.'

The following afternoon, when Donague was out, George and Donald went up to the room.

Apart from the fact that it was dusty and the furniture decaying, the room seemed quite ordinary. Donald Geary walked in. George French followed, but then the temperature dropped suddenly and a glowing ball of pink light appeared over the rocking-chair in the centre of the room. The ball of light grew larger and larger, until the whole room appeared bathed in a bright fire. The furniture began to vibrate and the rocking chair was swaying back and forth ominously.

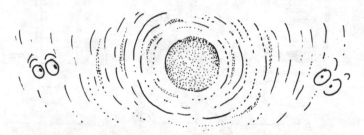

Suddenly Donald grabbed his neck and screamed. Something was trying to strangle him. He was struggling desperately with the unseen force which was pushing him down to the floor, when George rushed into the room to help his friend. As he pulled him to the door the glow diminished and the room became warm again.

As Donald recovered in the corridor, George locked the door. They returned the key to the desk drawer and vowed not to be so sceptical in the future.

The Unknown Warrior

The ghost of a bloodstained soldier from the First World War has been seen in Westminster Abbey, London. No one knows whether or not he has any connection with the memorial tomb of the Unknown Warrior, which lies in the abbey.

Grey Man of Macdhui

At least two people are said to have died of fright when they encountered the 'Grey Man of Macdhui'. The appearance of this spectre on the highest mountain in the Cairngorms, Scotland, is often accompanied by the sound of pounding hooves. He sometimes shouts at people in a loud and terrifying voice and he chases people who run away from him.

Battle in the Moonlight

Late one night in April, 1980, Mr and Mrs Reeves were returning to their country house at Holme Hale in Norfolk. Suddenly they found themselves in the middle of a ghostly battle. They could hear the terrifying cries of men as they were struck down, and the clash of arms rang out in the clear night air. The couple pinned themselves against a wall, for the noise was terrifying. But, although the area was clearly lit by bright moonlight, they could see nothing. When, after a few minutes, the noises died away, all the dogs in the locality suddenly began to bark and howl.

When she had recovered from the shock of this ghostly happening, Mrs Reeves became intrigued by what she and her husband had experienced and she decided to investigate. She discovered that there had been an uprising by peasants against the gentry in the same area during the 1600s. It seems that Mr and Mrs Reeves had been part of a ghostly re-enactment of that very battle.

The Severed Hand

Trumpet Major Blandford was a 19th-century Dragoon guard who was caught poaching by gamekeepers at Cranborne Chase in Dorset. There was a bloody fight in which one of the gamekeepers was killed. Blandford managed to escape, but his hand was severed in the fight. The hand was buried at Pimperne churchyard in Dorset, where its ghostly form has been seen, searching for the rest of the body.

The Door that was not There

In 1977, two sentries at Windsor Castle, Berkshire, England, saw the ghost of King Henry VIII walking along the battlements. He appeared to walk through a wall, and then he vanished. When old plans of the castle were checked, it was found that there had, in fact, been a door at that spot in days gone by.

Shipwreck

S oon after the start of the Second World War, a guard on watch on the East Goodwin lightship in southern England saw an old-fashioned paddle steamer run aground on the treacherous Goodwin Sands. The guard called the Ramsgate lifeboat station, and a lifesaving crew sped to the scene. The whole area was searched, but there was no sign of any wreckage or casualties. When the guard related how the shipwreck occurred, it came to light that he had witnessed the sinking of the *SS Violet* – a steamer that had gone down many years before!

The Black Nun

A ghost called the Black Nun is often seen at the Bank of England in the City of London. She is said to be searching for her brother who worked at the bank and who was sentenced to death for forgery.

The Green Lady of Mey

T he East Tower of the Queen Mother's private residence, the Castle of Mey, is visited by a ghost known as the Green Lady. The daughter of a 16th-century earl of Caithness, this unfortunate girl made the tragic mistake of falling in love with a humble ploughman. Her father was furious and locked her up in a room in the east wing to prevent her from ever seeing the man she loved again. Heartbroken, she lost interest in life and hurled herself to her death from an upstairs window. Her troubled spirit has haunted the castle ever since.

Ghost in a Grey Robe

A ghost in a grey robe has often been seen at Hampton Court Palace near London. She is the ghost of Mistress Sybil Penn, who was the nurse to Prince Edward, the son of Jane Seymour and Henry VIII.

Murder in the Theatre

Charles Maklin was a famous 18th-century actor who killed another actor named Hallam at the Theatre Royal, Drury Lane, London. Macklin was charged with murder but the charge was reduced to manslaughter and he lived to the age of 107. Since his death a thin, ugly ghost has occasionally been seen near the orchestra pit at Drury Lane Theatre. The description of the ghost fits Charles Macklin exactly.

The Handless Girl

Rait Castle in Nairnshire, Scotland, is haunted by the ghost of a handless girl in a bloodstained dress. It is said that she is the spirit of a girl who had her hands chopped off by the chief of her clan (a Scottish tribe) because she fell in love with a boy from a rival clan.

The Houseproud Ghost

In 1975, the Usher family of Bow in East London were amazed by the antics of a ghost in their house. She would slam doors and often cause a terrible commotion. She was also very abusive at times, especially to a psychic investigator who was called in to get rid of her. The ghost did have one useful trait however — she enjoyed doing the housework. The Ushers did not have to make the beds, tidy their cupboards or clean the bathroom — the ghost did it all for them.

Bull of Death

Brothers Zack and Gill Spencer had been rounding up cattle in Brewster County in Texas, USA. They began to argue over which of them owned one particularly fine looking animal. Zack allowed himself to get carried away. He shot at his brother and killed him. When he realized what he had done, Zack was grief-stricken.

A cowboy asked how the animal should be branded. 'Brand him "murderer", just like me,' said Zack, 'and then set him loose, and I hope he haunts the prairies for ever.' Zack then buried his brother and shot himself.

From that day in 1890, right through to about 1920, reports of people seeing the bull appeared throughout the land. It was said that everyone who saw it was cursed to become a killer or be killed. It seems that Zack's curse had come true.

A Ghostly Rescue

During the summer of 1965, Peter and Irene Nierman moored their barge near Tertogenbosch in Holland. One day, while Peter was ashore, their five-year-old son, Willem, fell into the water. Irene screamed, but there was nothing she could do to save the boy. Her husband was ashore and she was expecting another child. Some workmen heard her cries but they were too far away to prevent the boy from drowning in the fast-flowing waters. Then suddenly a dark-haired man appeared at the water's edge. Within seconds he was in the water alongside the boy, cradling him in his arms.

Although she had been watching him since he first appeared, Irene had not actually seen the man jump into the water. But she did not think about that at the time, for she was so relieved to have her son back safe and sound. She ran ashore to thank the stranger, but by the time she reached her son the man was already walking away towards a nearby warehouse. When she looked again, he had disappeared. By now the dockers, who had heard her cries, were on the scene and they asked Irene why she was looking at the warehouses. When she described the person who had rescued Willem the dockers

suddenly became very quiet and asked no more about the incident.

The next day Peter Nierman tried to find Willem's rescuer so he could thank him. After many hours of searching and asking questions, he discovered that the man who had saved his son's life was well-known in the area. He was Johan Udink, a dock-worker who had drowned at that very spot – 10 years before.

Haunting of Harecastle Tunnel

Harecastle Tunnel carries the Trent and Mersey Canal through Harecastle Hill, in northern England. In days gone by, barges would travel many miles out of their way to avoid going through the 4-kilometre (2½-mile)-long tunnel. It was, they said, haunted by the headless ghost of Kit Crewbucket, who was murdered and dumped in the canal.

Ghost of Grace

O n 7 September, 1838, the steamship, *Forfarshire*, was wrecked on the Harcar rocks about 1½ kilometres (1 mile) from the Longstone lighthouse, off the coast of Northumberland, northern England. The lighthouse keeper, William Darling, and his daughter, Grace, rescued several men from the sinking vessel. Grace Darling became a national heroine, but she died of tuberculosis just four years later. Since then, the ghost of Grace Darling has been seen many times in the Longstone lighthouse.

Beloved Dog

A small black dog was spotted by a policeman on duty at Didsbury, Manchester, England, in 1957. It was a moonlit night, and he saw the dog quite clearly in the garden of an old house. The dog walked across the lawn and then disappeared behind a tree. When the dog did not emerge from behind the tree, the

policeman went to investigate. At the base of the tree was a stone on which was written: 'Paddy. Died 2 September, 1913' — it was the gravestone of a dog.

His Lordship's Ghost

A phantom coach has often been seen in Greenwich on the south bank of the River Thames, London. The coach is heading towards the Ship and Billet Inn, where it then stops and collects its ghostly passenger, Lord John Angerstein, who died in the early 19th century.

His Lordship lived at Vanburgh Hill, Greenwich, in a life of luxury. It seems that luxury has even followed him into death, for when sighted, his ghost is well-dressed, in a black velvet suit and silver-buckled shoes.

The Mummy's Curse

In 1910, Douglas Murray, an Englishman, bought an ancient Egyptian mummy-case in Cairo. The case had contained the mummified body of a princess who had lived in Thebes in 1600 BC. Just a few hours after he had purchased the case, the American who had sold it to him died mysteriously. Following the American's death, Douglas Murray learned that the princess had been a member of a powerful religious cult and she had placed a dreadful curse on anyone who dared to disturb her final resting place.

Murray was an experienced Egyptologist and he had heard many stories of curses, so he paid very little attention. But then, a few days later, he was on a shooting expedition when his gun went off in his hands. He was so badly injured that his arm had to be amputated from the elbow. Then, on the journey back to England, two of Murray's companions died suddenly. A few months later, two of his Egyptian workers also died in mysterious circumstances.

Murray decided that he must get rid of the accursed mummy-case, and a lady offered to buy it from him. Almost immediately, her mother died, and then her boyfriend left her. When, eventually, she fell desperately ill, her lawyer persuaded her to return the mummy-case to Douglas Murray.

Murray presented the case to the British Museum, where a photographer and an Egypt-ologist both suddenly died. Finally, a New York museum agreed to take the case and it was shipped to America on a new, 'unsinkable' ship – called the *Titanic*. The *Titanic* hit an iceberg and sank, taking with her almost 1500 people – and the dreaded mummy's curse.

Footprint of Blood

On Christmas Eve, 1684, William Blatt's family were at home at Oakwell Hall, Birstall, West Yorkshire, when they saw William walking up the staircase towards the main bedroom. They were somewhat taken aback, for William Blatt was supposed to be in London at the time.

Blatt's wife and children ran up the stairs after him, but, at the top of the staircase, there was no one there. All that could be seen was a single footprint on the floor — it was of fresh blood. William Blatt had, in fact, been cruelly murdered that very evening — in London.

The Apparition of Powis Castle

In the 18th century, the ghost of a man in a gold laced hat often appeared in Powis Castle in Wales. He tried to communicate with the people in the castle but no one took any notice. One day he appeared before a woman while she was spinning, and managed to persuade her to follow him.

He led her to a neighbouring room where he instructed her to lift some floorboards. In a hole under the floorboards she discovered a heavy, locked box. She soon found the key, hidden in a crevice in the wall.

The strange man told the woman that the box and the key must be sent to the Earl of Powis, who was, at the time, in London. The woman did as she was told, and received a handsome reward from the Earl for finding the box. No one saw the strange man in the castle ever again.

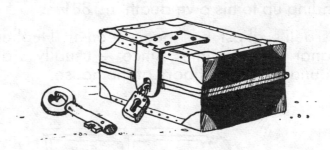

Phantom Coach

E ach Christmas, at Penryn in Cornwall, England, a phantom coach, drawn by headless horses, is said to appear. But everyone who has seen the spectre has vanished from the face of the earth within a few hours.

Haunting at Hughenden

T he British Prime Minister, Benjamin Disraeli (1804-81) bought Hughenden Manor, Buckinghamshire, in the summer of 1848. Almost every year from then on, Disraeli and his wife, Mary Anne, retired to the house when Parliament was in recess.

The Disraelis were happy at Hughenden — until Mrs Disraeli died in 1872. But Disraeli still loved the house and often stayed there in the months leading up to his own death in 1881.

Disraeli's ghost has been seen in Hughenden Manor several times since — usually walking around the upper floors of the house.

Reserved for a Ghost

A chair is reserved at the Busby Stoop Inn at Sandhutton, just south of Northallerton, north Yorkshire. It is reserved for the ghost of Tom Busby.

Tom Busby was hanged in 1702, for killing his father-in-law. The gallows, on which Busby was hanged, stood at the crossroads opposite the inn, and Tom Busby's ghost has often been seen with the hangman's noose tied around his neck!

Patrolling Policeman

P olice Sergeant Goddard hanged himself in one of the cells of London's Vine Street Police Station early this century. He has haunted the Metropolitan Police ever since. Many policemen have heard him patrolling the corridors at Vine Street Station. He also opens cell doors, and has been known to open desks and examine papers.

The Ghostly Workmen

Glamis Castle in the Vale of Strathmore is said to be the most haunted building in Scotland. Queen Elizabeth, the Queen Mother, who lived there as a girl admits that it is 'rather creepy in places'.

When she was young, the future Queen, then Lady Elizabeth Bowes-Lyon, slept, for a while, in the Blue Room in the castle. But, eventually, she asked her father, the 14th Earl of Strathmore, if she could sleep somewhere else. She said that the noise of the workmen kept her awake at night and she just could not put up with their constant banging and thumping day and night.

Her father moved her to another room immediately, for he knew there were no workmen in the house. The noises that the young Lady Elizabeth Bowes-Lyon had heard were caused by some of the many ghosts that haunt the ancient building.

Spectre of Speke

S peke Hall is a beautiful timbered house on the north bank of the River Mersey, about 12 kilometres (8 miles) south-east of Liverpool in the north of England. The Tapestry Room of the Hall, which is owned by The National Trust, is haunted by the sad ghost of Lady Beauclark.

When her husband, Topham Beauclark told his wife that he was financially ruined, Lady Beauclark became so distraught that she threw her baby out of the window of the Tapestry Room. She then killed herself in the Great Hall. Her tormented ghost has haunted the Hall ever since.

The Ghost of Cheam

A man, dressed in 16th-century costume, haunts Cheam in Surrey, in southern England. It is the ghost of Lancelot Andrews who was created Bishop of Winchester in 1619. He lived in a quiet rectory in Cheam and his ghost still haunts the area. But the unusual thing about this ghost is that it is visible only from the knees upwards. This is said to be due to the fact that the level of the floor has changed through the years since his death in 1626.

Ghosts' Walk

T he ghosts of Lady Margaret Massing-bred and her lover frequently walk along a path at Gunby Hall. This house, 10 kilometres (6 miles) west of Skegness in Lincolnshire, England, was built by Sir William Massing-bred, Lady Margaret's father, in 1700.

According to tradition, Lady Margaret fell in love with one of Sir William's employees, but her father forbade them to see each other. The couple planned to elope, but Sir William shot the man dead, and Lady Margaret died of grief.

Hauntings at Hailsham

I n 1969, two visitors to Michelham Priory, near Hailsham, Sussex, had the surprise of their life. They were in the Tudor Room of the 13th-century building, when a strange man in a cloak suddenly appeared. The appearance in itself was strange, but what was even stranger was that he was hovering up near the ceiling!

The ghost then descended to the floor and was followed by the apparition of a woman dressed in Tudor clothing.

The Vanishing Hitch-hiker

Many people have stopped to give a ride to a hitch-hiker at Frome, Somerset in the west of England. The hitch-hiker, who always wears a checked sports jacket, asks to be driven to Nunney Catch — but by the time they get there he has disappeared!

Ghostly Hands

For almost 70 years, a pair of ghostly hands have been scaring people travelling across the Devon moors. In the 1920s, the phantom hands overturned many pony traps. More recently, people have had the steering wheel of their car plucked from their grasp. A local resident, Florence Warwick, actually saw the hands clambering across the windscreen of her car. They disappeared when she screamed in terror.

Investigations in Enfield

I n 1977, psychical experts, reporters and even the Police were invited to a council house in Enfield, Middlesex to investigate strange happenings. Mrs Peggy Hodgson and her four children were being pestered by a poltergeist and they wanted an end to their problems.

The investigators reported instances of furniture moving in the house and toy bricks thrown about the rooms. A photographer from the *Daily Mirror* newspaper was hit on the forehead by a flying brick. There were also mysterious rapping noises. Investigators were unable to come up with any logical explanation for the phenomenon.

Finally, a psychical researcher, Maurice Grosse, managed to communicate with the unwanted 'house guest'. The poltergeist was thought to be the ghost of Bill Hobbs, who had died many years previously in the house. Hobbs had apparently come back from Durant's Park graveyard to see his family and was angry when he found that they no longer lived there.

Black Shuck

Black Shuck is a phantom dog that roams East Anglia in England. He is extremely large; foam and fire drip from his jaws, and he has one eye in the centre of his forehead.

The Brown Lady

Rayham Hall in Norfolk, England, is haunted by a sad ghost. She is known as The Brown Lady, because of the brocaded brown dress she is said to wear.

The ghost is thought to be that of Dorothy Walpole. When Dorothy and her husband were divorced, she was forbidden ever to see her children and died heartbroken. Even in death, her restless spirit paces about the Hall in search of them.

Most Haunted House in Britain

The ghosts of Borley Rectory made it the most famous haunted house of all time. A mysterious coach and horses used to gallop along the deserted roads leading to the house on the Suffolk/Essex borders. A girl dressed in white would flit through the building, and a ghostly nun was seen walking in the grounds. Bells rang of their own accord and objects flew through the air. Even after the house was burned down, people reported seeing mysterious figures at the windows of the gutted building.

Submarine Spook

On 21 January, 1918, three officers were standing on the bridge of the German submarine *U-65* when they spotted a man standing near the bows. Where he had come from they could not imagine for the submarine had only just surfaced. The officers shouted to the man, but when he turned to look up at the bridge, the three officers received a shock — glaring at them was Lieutenant Forster, who had been killed a few months before. The ghost stared at the men for a minute or so, then vanished as suddenly as he had appeared.

The Man in Grey

Dressed in an 18th-century riding cloak, riding boots, a three-cornered hat and carrying a sword, the Man in Grey haunts the Theatre Royal in Drury Lane, London. He is unusual for a ghost, for he walks only in the daytime. Because of this, hundreds of people have seen him.

Ghostly Monks

Two ghostly monks, one short and fat, the other tall and thin, have been seen on several occasions at Chingle Hall, Preston, Lancashire, in England. They are always seen deep in silent prayer.

The Girl who Vanished

O n 13 July, 1974, Maurice Goodenough was driving up Bluebell Hill in Kent, southern England, when suddenly, the figure of a young girl appeared in his headlights. He braked as hard as he could, but he was not quick enough and the car hit the girl. Goodenough jumped out of the car and ran over to where she was lying. She had serious head injuries, so he carried her to the roadside and covered her with a blanket before driving to the police station.

The police dashed to the scene of the accident, but when they arrived all they found was the blanket. The girl had vanished. Tracker dogs were used to find her, but without success.

Later, the driver discovered that other drivers had seen the girl on other occasions. Some had even given her a ride, but each time, she had vanished. Apparently, two girls had been killed at that spot in 1967. Perhaps one of them had come back as a ghost to haunt the living!

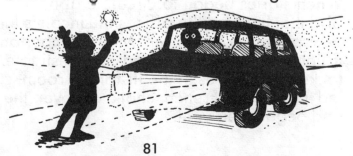

Claws of Terror

A group of men were standing near the lodge of the legal offices at Lincoln's Inn, London on the evening of 25 February, 1913, when they heard a terrified scream. They looked up and saw, silhouetted in a window, the figure of a man fighting off an invisible assailant.

They rushed up the stairs to the first floor office but they were too late – Charles Appleby, a young barrister, lay dead on the floor, covered in blood.

In the months that followed, a number of other tenants occupied the offices, but they all left because of the evil atmosphere that was present. A short while later, another barrister, John Radlett, was found hanged in the same office where Charles Appleby had been found. There were deep scratches on the inside of his locked door. They looked as if they had been made by the claws of an enormous bird.

When stories began to circulate about the ghost bird that haunted the offices in Lincoln's Inn, two newspaper editors, Sir Max Pemberton and Ralph Blumenfeld, decided to investigate. They locked themselves in the ill-famed room, sprinkled powdered French chalk all over the floor and began their vigil.

The two men spent the evening playing cards, and by midnight, they were getting bored with the whole idea. It seemed obvious that nothing untoward was going to happen. They were about to leave, when the locked door swung open. The windows, which had been bolted, opened by themselves, and a harsh wind entered the room, extinguishing the gaslight.

There was an horrific beating noise which sounded like the flapping of enormous wings. In the dim light the two men could just see a large, dark object moving across the room and out through a wall. Then the noise stopped, and the light came on again.

A reporter, who had been waiting downstairs and heard the commotion, rushed into the room, and all three men stared in disbelief at the floor. In the chalk, running from the centre of the room to the corner, were a set of gigantic claw marks!

A few years later the building was demolished and the giant bird, if that is what it was, was never heard of again.

Ghost Performer

During the performance of a play presented at a theatre in Wallington, Surrey, in 1973, many people in the audience were puzzled as to why one actor had remained in the shadows during the performance and had taken no active part in the proceedings.

This puzzled the producer even more, for he had not cast any such actor in his play. Furthermore, the doorway in which people saw the man standing, did not even exist!

The ghost appeared on subsequent evenings, and 24 people from four performances said they saw him. Everyone who described him said he was dressed in 16th-century clothing. But who the man was, and why he wanted to take part in the performance, remains a mystery.

The Flying Dutchman

T he *Flying Dutchman* is the most famous ghost ship in the world. It is usually seen around the Cape of Good Hope, South Africa, and is said to be the ghost of a Dutch ship lost in a storm during the 16th century.

There have been many recorded sightings of the *Dutchman*, but the most impressive one was made by Prince George (later George V) and his brother, Prince Albert, in July, 1881. The princes described the apparition they saw as 'a strange red light as of a phantom ship all aglow, in the midst of which light the mast, spars and sails of a brig 200 yards [180 metres] distant stood out in strong relief.'

Queen Victoria at Osborne

T he ghost of Queen Victoria, who died in 1901, has been seen walking through the grounds of Osborne House on the Isle of Wight. Osborne House was the Queen's home during her later years.

Haunted by a Highwayman

Many people travelling along the road towards Datchworth in Hertfordshire, England, claim to have heard the sound of a ghost-horse's hooves. The horse is said to belong to an 18th-century pieman, called Clibbon, who was beaten to death by local farmers when they discovered that he was a highwayman.

Today, a wooden post by the roadside marks the spot of this dastardly deed and Clibbon's horse can be heard dashing away from his pursuers along the road.

Lady in Grey

The Theatre Royal at Bath, Avon, is haunted by a lady in grey, who watches the performance from one of the boxes.

The Phantom Piper

As dawn broke on 1 July, 1916, during the Battle of the Somme, the British soldiers were in their trenches ready for the advance. They were going to have to cross no-man's land in an attempt to break through the German lines – a job that was going to be far from easy.

Suddenly, a Scottish piper appeared, walking bravely along the edge of the trench, in full view of the enemy. The spirits of the British soldiers were lifted by the piper's display of courage, and seconds later they were advancing through the mud towards enemy lines.

A few months later, names were being submitted for awards for valour at the Battle of the Somme. A Victoria Cross was proposed for the valiant Scottish piper, but exhaustive searches failed to discover who he was or what regiment he could have belonged to.

It seemed that it was a ghost that had led the men into battle that day.

Pity Poor Bradford

The Duke of Newcastle occupied Bolling Hall at Bradford, Yorkshire, during the English Civil War (1642-49). One day, he ordered that all Roundhead prisoners were to be executed the next morning. But he changed his mind that night, when he saw the spectre of a woman in white. She was standing near his bed, wringing her hands and saying, 'Pity poor Bradford!' The Duke did, indeed, take pity on Bradford. The prisoners' lives were spared.

Water, Water, Everywhere

In Stuhlingen, West Germany, Elsa Arndt found a small puddle of water on her dining-room floor. She assumed that one of her daughters had spilled it accidentally and mopped it up. But then she found a pool of water on her bed and some more on the bathroom floor.

Elsa believed that her daughters were playing a trick — until water began gushing from the walls! Her husband, Irvin, called in a plumber, but the plumber could find nothing wrong with the plumbing system.

When, one day, blobs of water actually appeared in mid-air the Arndt family decided to approach Hans Bender, who was well known in Germany for his psychic investigations. Bender first turned off the water supply to the house at the mains, but still the water came. In one test, Bender had a bedroom completely sealed up, even going to the extent of blocking the keyhole, but when Hans Bender re-opened the room there was a pool of water on the floor.

After three weeks, with water appearing in the house up to 60 times each day, the water suddenly stopped coming. Hans Bender came to the conclusion that the water had been caused by a poltergeist trying to contact twelve-year-old Sabine Arndt, Elsa's daughter.

Ghost at Buckingham Palace

Major John Gwynne was a secretary to King Edward VII, who reigned from 1901 to 1910. Gwynne shot himself at his desk one day in the Palace. His ghost has been seen sitting at the desk many times since.

The Black Dog of Blythburgh

The parson of Blythburgh in Sussex, England, was reading his sermon on 4 August, 1557, when he was suddenly interrupted by a crash of thunder. A flaming arrow pierced the church wall and the church bell crashed to the ground, followed by tumbling masonry. The congregation was terrified, but there was more horror to come: a great black hound of massive proportions came rushing through the church, attacking people as it went.

The hound vanished and was never seen again, but its burnt and blackened paw marks can still be seen on the old church door.

Headless Cyclist

As he walked towards the Fox and Hounds Inn near Northampton one winter's day in 1940, George Dobbs saw a car coming along the snow-bound road. Approaching the car, from the opposite direction, was a man on a bicycle. The man appeared to have no head.

The car driver did not seem to see the cyclist, but continued to head straight towards him. Within seconds the car had passed. George was convinced that the cyclist must have been hit, and he ran over to help. But the cyclist was nowhere to be seen!

When he arrived at the inn Dobbs told his friends about his strange experience. Then one of his friends, the local gravedigger, said, 'There was an accident at that spot 25 years ago. A cyclist was knocked off his bike in deep snow – the accident severed his head.'

Cantering through Chiddingstone

The ghost-woman on horseback, who frequents the village of Chiddingstone, in Kent, is quite unusual. This is because she is normally seen in daylight, riding through the village. She is said to be the ghost of Lady Ann Streatfield, who lived in the local manor house in the 18th century.

Where There's a Will

Nine days after his father's death in May, 1948, Leslie Freedman had a strange dream. In the dream he saw his father, Leonard, sitting at his office desk. His father turned towards him and said, 'I want you to call all the family together at 7 o'clock on Saturday.'

Leslie Freedman was not sure what to do about his dream, but he called the family together as requested — although he dared not tell anyone the reason for the gathering.

By 6.50 pm everyone had arrived at the house and they sat in the dining-room next to the library, and waited for Leslie Freedman to explain why he had called the meeting.

Suddenly, the whole family found themselves looking through the open door into the library. There, looking at some books, was the ghost of Leonard Freedman. The spectre pointed to one of the books and then vanished.

It was Leslie's brother, Arthur, who moved first. He went into the library and took out the book which the phantom had pointed to. It was *A History of Lighthouses on the Irish Coast*.

Arthur flicked through the pages in curious amazement. Inside the front cover was Leonard Freedman's last will and testament – a document that the family had been searching for ever since his death.

The Girl in White

The 14th-century George and Dragon Inn, at West Wycombe, in Berkshire, is haunted by a female ghost dressed in white. Apparently, a woman was attacked and killed by a vicious gang of men in one of the upstairs rooms and it is her ghost that haunts the inn.

Ghosts of the Goodwins

Goodwin Sands, off the Kent coast, are reputed to be haunted by many of the vessels that have floundered on these treacherous sandbanks. The three-masted schooner, *Lady Lovibond*, was lost with all hands in 1748, but a ghost of the vessel has been seen at 50-year intervals ever since. If the apparition keeps to this strange and inexplicable schedule, she will make her next ghostly appearance in 1998. But the *Lady Lovibond* is only one of several shipwrecked vessels that haunt this area. Many other sightings will be reported before the *Lady Lovibond* makes her next scheduled appearance.

The Haunted Bolero

F or the play, *The Queen Came By*, at the Duke of York Theatre in London, actress, Thora Hird, had to wear a long dress topped with an embroidered velvet bolero jacket. Whenever she wore it she experienced a choking sensation. Her understudy experienced the same sensation when she wore it, as did the stage manager and the director's wife.

The jacket proved to be quite a problem. Three mediums were called in, but to no avail. Three members of the cast were asked to try the jacket and two of them felt as if they were being choked by it.

After some research into the history of the jacket, a Victorian original, it was discovered that the owner had been throttled to death by her lover while wearing it. She had haunted the garment ever since.

Death in Bed

On the night of 31 May, 1810, the Duke of Cumberland had returned to St James's Palace, London, after a visit to the opera, when his valet, Sellis, tried to kill him. The attempt was unsuccessful, and, later that night, Sellis committed suicide.

That, at least, was the duke's version of events on that fateful night. However, it was not long before rumours began to circulate that Sellis had, in fact, been blackmailing the Duke of Cumberland and that the duke had actually murdered Sellis.

It seems that this rumour may well have been the truth, and the Duke of Cumberland's version of events a lie. For, since that night, the valet's ghost has been seen several times – sitting up in his bed with his throat cut!

The Dead Seamen

On 1 December, 1929, James Courtney and Michael Meehan were killed by fumes whilst working below deck on the oil tanker *Waterton*. The following day they were buried at sea. On 3 December the two men were seen swimming alongside the ship! There was no doubt that they were the dead men and they stayed alongside for three days.

Captain Tracy of the *Waterton* reported the incident to his office in New Orleans when they docked there. He was issued with a camera just in case the men should reappear on the next voyage. And reappear they did. The captain managed to take several photographs of them. When the pictures were developed, both men were clearly visible on the prints.

Queen in her Chariot

The warrior queen, Boudicca, who led the Iceni tribe against the Romans, has been seen on countless occasions riding in her chariot at Cammeringham near Lincoln, in the north of England.

Britain's Most Haunted Village

Pluckley in Kent, in the south of England, is said to be Britain's most haunted village. It is believed to have no fewer than 12 ghosts. These include the Red Lady, searching for her lost baby, the White Lady who glides through the library of Surrenden Dering manor house, and a horse-drawn coach that careers down the village street. There is also the ghost of an old pipe-smoking gypsy woman, a phantom schoolmaster who hanged himself, and the black shape of a miller. It is also said that the ghost of a colonel who hanged himself walks through the woods, and terrible screams are heard near the railway station where a man was smothered to death. A phantom monk has been sighted at a house called Greystones, a ghostly lady haunts Rose Court, and a mysterious modern ghost inhabits the church of St Nicholas. At the appropriately named Fright Corner, the gory death of a highwayman who was killed by a sword and speared to a tree is said to be re-enacted every night.

A Fatal Mistake

The Fleur de Lys Inn at Norton St Philip, Somerset in the west of England, has been haunted for the past 300 years, ever since an innocent passer-by was tragically killed there. The man arrived at the inn to find that an execution of rebels, who had supported the Duke of Monmouth's uprising in 1685, was about to take place behind the premises. As he opened the gate to let the men through to the execution site, he was pushed into their midst by a guard. He was hanged by mistake, and his ghost is a constant reminder of his untimely and unfortunate death.

The Severed Hand

Whilst he was visiting Luxor, Egypt in 1890, Count Luis Hamon was called upon to attend a prominent Arab sheik. Hamon was well-known as a psychic healer and he had been asked to cure the sheik of malaria. This he did, and the grateful sheik gave him an unusual gift in return. It was the mummified hand of an ancient Egyptian princess.

The princess's hand had been cut off by her father, King Akhnaton, in an argument. Hamon offered the hand to various museums, but no one was willing to accept it, so it was eventually locked away in the safe in Hamen's London home. It remained there for over 30 years, until, one day, in 1922, Count Hamon's wife opened the safe to find that the hand was no longer shrivelled. Its appearance had changed to a healthy-looking living hand.

The Countess insisted that the hand should be disposed of immediately, and her husband readily agreed. It was decided that the hand should be given a proper funeral, out of respect for the dead princess. This was arranged for the night of 31 October. During the funeral service, Count Hamon laid the hand in the fireplace and then read a passage from the *Egyptian Book of the Dead*. Suddenly, there was a clap of thunder and a blast of wind blew open the door to the sitting-room.

In the doorway was the figure of a woman dressed in the traditional clothes of an Egyptian princess. Her right arm had been severed. The figure approached the fireplace, bent over towards the hand and then vanished.

When the Count and Countess recovered sufficiently from their fright, they searched the fireplace. The hand had vanished, and it was never seen again.

Thanks for Drivers

The ghost of Nance is often seen by lorry drivers travelling to York in northern England. She runs alongside the moving lorries, and if there is any danger ahead, she slows them down to warn them.

Nance was an 18th-century farmer's daughter who left her fiancé to marry a highwayman. But the highwayman was already married. He left Nance pregnant and penniless. Nance's ex-fiancé, a coach driver, found her several months later, standing on the York road nursing her baby. He took her home to care for her, but both she and the baby died. Because of the coach driver's kindness, Nance's ghost has been helping drivers ever since.

Ghost in the Tower

A soldier on guard duty at the Tower of London, in 1864, saw a ghostly white figure glide towards him through a doorway. The sentry challenged the figure. Receiving no reply, he stabbed at it with his bayonet — but the

steel met no resistance. The guardsman let out a yell and fainted – he had just realized he was facing a ghost.

When the Captain of the Guard found the man senseless on the ground, he was charged with sleeping on duty. At the court martial it seemed certain he would be sentenced, but two witnesses came forward – they too had seen the white figure. Other guards then added that they had seen ghostly figures whilst on duty in the same part of the Tower, and the guardsman was finally acquitted.

The Lady and her Dog

E ver since the 13th century, a lady with a small dog has often been seen at Michelham Priory near Hailsham, Sussex. Whenever they are approached, they disappear.

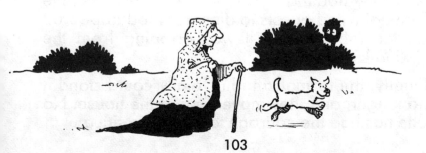

Blood from the Ceiling

When an American farmer, called Walingham, discovered a skeleton in his new house in Oakville, Ohio, USA, he threw the bones in a lime kiln. It was an action he was soon to regret. Doors in the house suddenly began to slam shut, furniture moved mysteriously across the floor, and mysterious bells began to chime incessantly. One day, Walingham's dog started barking furiously and throwing himself about the room. It seemed the dog was being attacked by an invisible assailant, for somehow the dog's neck became broken.

Ghostly groans were heard in the upstairs rooms of the house, and once a dismembered hand was seen floating down the staircase. When the farmer invited guests to dinner, blood appeared on the tablecloth – it was dripping from the ceiling.

Finally, the farmer and his family could stand it no longer, and they moved out of the house. No one has had the courage to live there since.

Ghostly Battle in the Sky

A group of farmhands were walking home from Banbury to Kineton, in Oxfordshire, when they saw an amazing scene at Edge Hill. There, in the sky above, was the Battle of Edge Hill – a battle which had been fought three months previously in October, 1642.

The terrified farmhands watched for two hours as soldiers marched across the sky, banners waving, swords glinting. Then suddenly, the scene disappeared.

The men reported what they had seen, and the following day, an investigating party was sent to Edge Hill, only to watch the ghostly battle re-enacted once again.

Later, Charles II sent six of his officers to investigate. They, too, saw the battle, and even recognized some of their comrades who had been killed.

Hell Hound

There is supposed to be treasure hidden in Clopton Hall, Stowmarket in Suffolk. However, it is difficult to find, for it is guarded by a ghostly creature that has the head of a dog and the body of a monk.

Ghost in the Road

Several drivers have swerved to avoid a woman in white at Barrow Gurney, near Bristol. But as soon as they have successfully avoided her, she disappears.

What, What?

Guests at Windsor Castle, one of the British Royal Family residences, have often heard the words, 'What, what?' during the night. It is the ghost of King George III, whose favourite phrase was: 'What, what?'.

Frenchmen in Devon

During the Napoleonic Wars in the 18th century, French prisoners of war were imprisoned in Dartmoor Prison in Devon. To this day, the ghosts of the French prisoners are still sometimes seen in the prison burial grounds.

Terror at Brockley

Samuel Trent and his family moved into their new house at Brockley, Kent, southern England, in the autumn of 1920. One night in December, a neighbour knocked at the door and said that someone was switching the lights on and off in the attic rooms. Trent went up to check, but found the attic in darkness.

The following night, his daughter's bed began to shake violently. When she switched on the light the room was full of mist.

A few days later, Trent was in the drawing-room when he heard his wife scream. He rushed upstairs to find her struggling with a pillow, which was being pressed against her face by an invisible force.

In the days that followed, furniture was thrown around the rooms, deep sighs were heard, and ornaments were lifted from the shelves and smashed to the ground. Mr Trent was attacked by something invisible, and Mrs Trent saw a strange black figure in the hallway.

The Trents moved out of the house, but although it remained empty for a year, neighbours still reported lights flashing on and off and strange bumps and knockings coming from inside the house.

In 1950, an architect moved into the house and soon discovered the house's grisly secret — behind a false wall in the cellar were the remains of a body. It was said to have been there for 100 years. Its identity was never discovered.

The Radiant Boy

The Radiant Boy is the ghost of a young boy who appears in Corby Castle, Cumberland in northern England. He is seen, dressed in white, in the oldest part of the castle. No one knows who he was, or how he came to haunt the castle ramparts.

Guardian of the Bomber

In 1977, the Lincoln bomber RF398 was taken to the RAF Aerospace Museum hangar at Cosford, Shropshire for repairs. It was not long before the men working on the plane began seeing a mysterious airman. He was always either in the hangar or standing on the wing of the plane, dressed in a leather jacket and white polo-necked sweater – a style popular with early aviators.

After a while, the men came to the conclusion that the phantom airman was protecting both the plane and the men who were working on it. One engineer fell backwards from the wing 4½ metres (15 feet) on to the concrete floor – but was completely uninjured. Another man walked into the sharp edge of a propeller and was also unhurt. Strange whistling was heard, and on a cold day, when there were icicles hanging from the roof, it was so cosy inside the plane that the men didn't even have to wear coats.

The repairmen never discovered who their strange protector had been, but they were glad of his company, all the same.

Catherine's Final Plea

C atherine Howard was the fifth wife of King Henry VIII. Two years after their marriage in 1540, the queen was arrested, accused of adultery and was sentenced to death. Shortly before her execution, she ran through the corridors of Hampton Court Palace, the Royal residence, to plead with the King to spare her life. Henry was unremitting, and on 13 February, 1542, Catherine was executed at the Tower of London. However, Catherine Howard's spirit never left Hampton Court – she has been seen on several occasions, gliding towards the king's chamber, seeking mercy from her husband.

Tightrope Rescue

P ierre Hurette was determined that he would perform his tightrope act at the Olympiadrome in Paris as planned. His doctors had advised him against it. He had been in hospital for four weeks following an accident on the high wire, in which his partner had been killed. Hurette's ribs were encased in tape and his arm was still heavily bandaged, but he was determined to follow the old show business tradition: 'the show must go on'.

Because of his injuries, Hurette found the climb to the high wire extremely painful, but he was determined to succeed. He began to walk across the wire. Each step was more painful than the last, and he faltered when he reached the half-way point. It was clear that the strain had proved too much and he was going to fall, when suddenly, another figure appeared on the high

112

wire. He steadied Hurette and then walked to the end of the wire where a rope was hanging. He brought the rope back to Hurette who grasped it desperately. The rope enabled Hurette to reach the end of the wire and then down to safety. When he looked up again, the mysterious figure had vanished.

It was not only Hurette who had recognized the figure that had saved his life on the high wire that summer's day. Many others recognized him as Paul de Champ, who had been Hurette's partner until the accident four weeks previously. Hurette had been badly injured in the fall, but de Champ was killed. The packed audience at the Olympiadrome had witnessed the amazing spectacle of a ghost saving the life of his former partner.

Darrell and his Hounds

Littlecote Manor in Wiltshire, southern England, was built between 1490 and 1520. It is a beautiful house in luscious surroundings – but it is also haunted.

One night in 1575, Mother Barnes, a midwife, was brought secretly to the house from the nearby village of Great Shefford to deliver a baby girl. The father, 'Wild' Darrell, last of the Darrell family, took the baby and threw her into the fire!

Darrell himself lived until 1598, when he was killed while hunting in the park at a place still known as Darrell's Style.

The ghosts of 'Wild' Darrell and his hounds still haunt the park, and the room in which the baby was killed is frequently visited by the ghosts of Mother Barnes, the baby and her mother.

The Skating Soldier

During the winter of 1814, a young army drummer fell in love with a girl who lived at Potter Heigham on the Norfolk Broads, England. The girl's father did not approve of their association, so the two lovers would meet in secret at a place called Swim Coots, on the edge of the Broads.

To get to the meeting place, the soldier used to skate across the frozen surface of the Broads. One evening, there had been a slight thaw. The ice gave way as the soldier was half way across, and he was drowned.

The soldier's ghost still haunts the place. At 7 o'clock on February evenings, the ghost skates through the mist to his romantic rendezvous.

Clanking Chains

Clanking chains accompany the cowled figure of a monk who haunts Buckingham Palace in London. The ghost is said to be that of a monk who was bound in chains and then left to die one Christmas.

Ghostly Faces on the Floor

O ne hot day in August, 1971, at Belmez in southern Spain, an old Spanish woman was working in her kitchen when she was startled by a shout from her granddaughter. When the woman turned round to see what the trouble was, she froze in horror. Staring up at her from the pink floor-tiles was a face.

The woman tried rubbing out the face with a rag, but this only resulted in the face opening its eyes wider, as if in great pain and sorrow.

The landlord of the house was called to examine the floor. He ripped up the floor-tiles and put down a new concrete floor. This seemed to solve the problem, but when, three weeks later, another face appeared on the new floor, the local authorities were alerted, and it was decided to dig up the entire kitchen.

Workmen had not been digging for long, when they discovered the source of the phantom face — the kitchen floor had been covering the remains of a medieval monastery.

It seems that the discovery of the ancient burial ground only released even more spirits. Ghostly faces began appearing all over the floor, even after more new tiles had been laid, and when the kitchen was eventually locked and sealed up,

the faces began appearing in other parts of the house.

A team of ghost-hunters installed sound equipment, which picked up the sounds of unearthly moaning and groaning, but, before a proper investigation could be undertaken, the sounds and the faces stopped, just as suddenly and mysteriously as they had started.

The Ghost of Raleigh

The Elizabethan discoverer, Sir Walter Raleigh is said to haunt the ruined castle at Sherborne, Dorset. He is often seen walking through what was once a garden, but when he reaches a tree called Raleigh's Oak, he suddenly disappears.

Spectre in the White House

When Queen Wilhelmina of the Netherlands was staying in the White House in 1905, she told President Roosevelt that she had seen the ghost of Abraham Lincoln in her bedroom. The President was not surprised at this, for his wife Eleanor had often sensed Lincoln's presence and his secretary, Mary Eben, had actually seen the dead president sitting in a chair and removing his boots!

Mystery in the Museum

The wartime B-29 bomber, *Raz'n Hell*, in the Castle Air Force Museum in California, USA, did not have any bulbs or batteries. No wonder the museum staff got a shock when the landing lights came on one day.

That was not the only strange occurrence on this plane. Locked doors have swung open of their own accord and a shadowy shape has been seen in the cockpit. Museum staff are convinced that the craft is haunted by the dead crew.

The Wet Ghost

Every so often, a man is seen emerging, soaking wet, from the moat of Scotney Castle at Lamberhurst in Kent in southern England. It is said to be the ghost of a customs official who was sent to arrest the owner of the castle. The customs man was murdered and thrown into the moat.

Horseman of Bottlebush Down

A ghostly horseman has been seen at Bottlebush Down, near the A3081 road between Cranborne and Sixpenny Handley in Dorset, southern England. One of the best documented sightings was made by R C Clay in 1924. Clay was an archaeologist and was able to identify the horseman, from his clothes, as dating from the Bronze Age. This makes the horseman of Bottlebush Down one of Britain's oldest ghosts.

The Garden Ghost

In 1938, soon after the Carr family moved into a vicarage in Wiltshire, England, a girl in white began making regular appearances. Ten-year-old Frances and seven-year-old Janet were the first to see her. They told their mother about the girl who would come close to them but run away when spoken to.

Mrs Carr thought her daughters were imagining things — until she saw the girl herself. One day, whilst sitting in the garden with a friend, Mrs Carr heard the gate open. A little girl, wearing a white dress, and carrying a small parcel, walked up the path and went into the house. A few minutes later, she re-emerged and walked away. When the housekeeper brought out a tray of tea Mrs Carr asked about the visitor — but the housekeepr knew nothing about the girl. None of the other servants had seen her either.

The girl in white was seen frequently after that. On most occasions she was on her own, but there were several times when she was seen with an old man. She was always crying when the man was with her.

The Carr family eventually left the vicarage, and after the Second World War the building lay derelict for a few years. It was finally pulled down in 1953. During the demolition, workmen found a cupboard that had been bricked up. Beneath the floorboards of the cupboard they found the skeleton of a young girl and the remnants of a white dress.

Racing Ghosts

Brooklands racetrack at Weybridge in Surrey ceased to be used for motor racing in the 1930s. But sounds of ghostly motor races have been heard there ever since.

The Cauld Lad

T he Cauld (Cold) Lad is the ghost of Hylton Castle in Sunderland, north-east England. Thought to be the ghost of a stable lad who was killed in the castle, he is rather an unusual ghost – he appears naked!

The Chocked Batallion

I n 1648, during the English Civil War, a group of Scottish soldiers were captured and executed by Oliver Cromwell's Roundheads at Newton-le-Willows, near Warrington, Lancashire. The Scots were nicknamed 'The Chocked Batallion', and to this day, the sounds of their footsteps are still to be heard near the site where they were killed.

Riding Across the Moors

The spirit of Sir Francis Drake is said to ride across Dartmoor, in Devon, with a ghostly pack of hounds alongside him. It is said that any dog who hears the hounds is destined to die immediately.

Captain George

Every year, thousands of people flock to the English seaside town of Penzance, the first Cornish town to become a holiday resort. A number of them take refreshment at the waterside tavern called The Dolphin. But very few of them know that The Dolphin is haunted.

The inn is visited by the ghost of a man wearing a three-cornered hat, and a coat with brass buttons. Local people call the ghost 'Captain George'. His appearance does resemble that of an Elizabethan sea-captain but no one knows why he haunts the inn.

I am Staying Here

Many people have heard the sound of a motor-cycle near Cloud's Hill, a country cottage in Dorset, England. It is believed to be the noise of the motor-cycle that belonged to T E Lawrence — Lawrence of Arabia — who led the Arab revolt of 1916.

In 1935, Lawrence wrote to a friend, Lady Astor, and mentioned his love for the cottage. 'Nothing,' he wrote, 'would take me away from Cloud's Hill. It is an earthly paradise and I am staying here.' Five days after writing this letter, he was killed in a motor-cycle accident. His words seem to have come true, for his ghost has been seen at Cloud's Hill several times since his death — often dressed in the Arab robes he used to wear in the desert.

Haunting at Happisburgh

H appisburgh (pronounced Haysborough) is a coastal village in Norfolk, in England. It was once the haunt of smugglers, and one smuggler still haunts the village. Every so often, the legless body of a man comes in with the tide at Well Corner in the village. At first sight the body also appears to be headless – but then the observer realizes that, although the head has been severed, it is still attached to the body by a few sinews – quite a gruesome sight!

This ghost was first seen in 1765. As it usually appeared at Well Corner, it was decided to search the well. Deep inside the well, the villagers found the decomposed body of a seaman, his head almost severed from the body – and he had no legs!